Managing Time

2O MINUTE MANAGER SERIES

Get up to speed fast on essential business skills. Whether you're looking for a crash course or a brief refresher, you'll find just what you need in HBR's 20-Minute Manager series—foundational reading for ambitious professionals and aspiring executives. Each book is a concise, practical primer, so you'll have time to brush up on a variety of key management topics.

Advice you can quickly read and apply, from the most trusted source in business.

Titles include:

Creating Business Plans

Delegating Work

Finance Basics

Getting Work Done

Giving Effective Feedback

Innovative Teams

Managing Projects

Managing Time

Managing Up

Performance Reviews

Presentations

Running Meetings

20 MINUTE MANAGER SERIES

Managing Time

Focus on what matters
Avoid distractions
Get things done

HARVARD BUSINESS REVIEW PRESS

Boston, Massachusetts

Copyright 2014 Harvard Business School Publishing Corporation

The web addresses referenced in this book were live and correct at the time of the book's publication but may be subject to change.

Library of Congress Cataloging-in-Publication Data

Managing time.
    pages cm. — (The 20-minute manager series)
    Includes index.
    ISBN 978-1-62527-224-9 (alk. paper)
    1. Time management.
    HD69.T54.M363 2014
    650.1'1—dc23

                                            2013050976

ISBN: 9781625272249
eISBN: 9781625272294

Preview

You have too much to do and too little time. It's frustrating and stressful and has a big impact on your success. Although you can't magically add more hours to the day, you can learn to manage your time—however limited it may be—more carefully and efficiently. This book will quickly teach you the basic steps and tools you can use to take control:

- Logging your time

- Prioritizing your responsibilities

- Developing a plan to reallocate your time to reflect your goals

- Managing deadlines

- Creating detailed, task-oriented to-do lists

- Avoiding interruptions and distractions

Contents

Contents

Managing Time

Why Manage
Your Time?

Why Manage Your Time?

Why do I never seem to have enough time to get everything done?

Do you find yourself asking that question frequently?

If so, you probably have a lot going on: There are your daily tasks and the big projects that your boss has put on your plate, not to mention new skills that you want to learn, and bigger goals that you'd like to accomplish. You're juggling a wide range of tasks, responsibilities, projects, and deadlines. You're swamped, and you're not sure if you can pull it all off. There's too much to do, too little time. There are only so many hours in a workweek, after all.

When time is scarce, and progress is slow, it can be overwhelming. And sometimes you just can't get everything done, and you miss a deadline or let a project fall away unfinished.

There's nothing more to do about it, right?

Wrong: Whether you're new to the work world or a veteran coping with a long-standing time-management issue, you can learn to prioritize, to plan, to be more efficient, and to align your schedules with your goals. The supra-organizational impulse need not be coded into your DNA; time management is a skill that you can learn and continue to fine-tune with practice. You just have to be disciplined.

There isn't a one-size-fits-all approach to time management, since we all have different schedules, responsibilities, and personalities. There are some best practices, however. This book will walk you through those basic, tried-and-true methods of getting your schedule back on track—and will do it fast, so you don't waste any (more) time.

You'll learn how to do the following:

- Assess how well you're spending your time now, uncovering the hidden time sinks in your day

- Clarify your goals so you can make sure to work toward them

- Reallocate your time to prioritize the work and goals that are important to you and your organization

- Overcome the common obstacles that keep you from doing the work that you *should* be doing

Once you get the hang of it, you'll find managing your time more deliberately to be well worth it. You'll have time and energy to focus on the skills, tasks, and projects that are most important to you, your boss, your team, and your organization.

Let's get started.

Assess Yourself

Assess Yourself

T he first step to effective time management is self-awareness.

You probably have a general sense of what types of tasks you perform on a daily basis, and how much time you spend on each. But perception isn't always reality, and you may overestimate or underestimate, and any blind spots you have won't help. Those miscalculations can add up and leave you with an incomplete picture of where your time is going.

That's why it's important to actually track your time. For a week or two, keep a log of the tasks that you perform and how much time you spend working on each. This chapter will show you how to put together a tracking plan and log that works for you.

It's true that time tracking can feel like busywork, but the minutes you spend on it can be kept to a minimum and it's the best way to get a clear and detailed account of how you've spent—and wasted—your time. The more aware you become of your habits, the more data you will have to make better time-management plans and decisions going forward.

State your objectives

Before you begin tracking your activities, identify the reason you're going through this exercise. What do you want to accomplish by better managing your time? This question may seem too simple to spend much time on (you don't have any time, after all!), but it's important because your answer will inform your efforts *and* serve as your metric for success. If you know where you want to end up, it's a lot easier to figure out how to get there.

Your goal could be personal or professional. You may have a new project that you want to make time for, a skill you want to acquire, or a performance metric your boss wants you to reach. Or you may want to stop missing deadlines set by your colleagues—or by your manager. Perhaps you want to stop feeling so much pressure to stay late and work when you could be home with your family. It may be a combination of these. Just make sure that your own goal as you state it matches up with those that your manager has set for you.

Break down your responsibilities

You'll want to make the time-tracking process as simple, painless, and manageable as possible.

To do this, break down your job duties into broad categories—for example, personal growth, employee management, core responsibilities, administrative work—and then track the amount of time that you spend doing tasks in each category. It's easier and more efficient than logging every single task that you spend time on.

You can also break down your duties along other lines, depending on the types of problems you face. If you work in a deadline-intensive environment, for example, you could break down your workload into short-term, long-term, and urgent tasks. Or by priority level: high, medium, low. We'll assume you're using the broad category method for the sake of this book, but any of these will work.

While it's more labor intensive, it may be beneficial to track your activities at a more detailed level for a week or two. You'll put more time into the tracking, but you'll be rewarded with more pockets of inefficient time that you uncover as a result of that detailed accounting. If, on the other hand, there's one category that's been a pain point for you—say, you seem to be spending an inordinate amount of time on administrative tasks—you may want to track only that category.

Here are some typical categories to track.

- *Core responsibilities.* These are the day-to-day tasks that make up the crux of your job. For a book editor, for example, core responsibilities include editing manuscripts and corresponding with authors. If you were at a party, and someone asked you what your day-to-day work entails, what would you say? The types of activities you would describe are most likely your core responsibilities.

- *Personal growth.* This category consists of the activities and projects that you find valuable, meaningful, and fulfilling but that may not be part of your everyday responsibilities. It could be a big project you've taken on, or a skill you'd like to learn. In a perfect world, most people would choose to devote a lot more time, focus, and energy to these activities because they contribute most to their career and personal development.

If you're feeling in a rut careerwise and aren't progressing as fast as you'd like, this is the best category to track. Do the same if you want to carve out time to learn a new skill.

- *Managing people.* Do you have any direct reports? Do you work collaboratively with colleagues? Lead a team? If so, the amount of time that you spend managing people—that team, your colleagues, even your superiors—should be logged here.

  If you feel that people issues are taking up a large chunk of your time, you could break this category down into smaller subcategories such as managing up (your boss and other superiors), managing across (your peers), and managing your direct reports.

- *Administrative tasks.* These are the necessary chores you perform each day: emails, time sheets, expense reports, approving invoices, and so forth.

- *Crises and fires.* Interruptions. Urgent matters. Unplanned meetings. Last-minute issues that need to be dealt with right away can sabotage even the best time-management plans. That's why they're particularly critical to track. Although you won't ever be able to anticipate when they're going to happen, if you can identify some patterns—for example, that you spend five hours a week on average putting out fires— you can plan accordingly.

- *Free time.* This may not be an official part of your duties, but everyone needs to take breaks from work. Lunch, a walk, a coffee pit-stop, a chat with a coworker, personal email, the internet—in small doses, these can unclutter your mind and even increase collaboration and productivity. But if you're not careful, these brief respites can add up.

As you break down your responsibilities, think carefully about what a typical day looks like at your job. You may find that you want to supplement or replace some of the categories above with some that are more specific to your role.

Track your time

Once you have your categories in place, you can build your time-tracking tool. If you're a pen-and-paper type of person, the tool described below should work well for you. If you're more digitally oriented, there are a host of time-tracking programs and apps that make the process simpler by doing most of the work and math for you. Either way, the same principles are at work and it's important to understand them.

Whether you decide to track one category or fifteen, it's important to be as diligent as possible. Log every hour. As you begin, you will want the most accurate and detailed data possible. Frankly, this can be a pain: Nobody wants to take time out of their busy schedule to remind themselves of how busy they are. But the more effort you put into time tracking, the more confident you'll be in your results and the more likely that you'll find a solution to your problem.

Here's how to build your time-tracking tool:

1. At the very start of a workweek, create a time chart as in table 1. Devote a row for each day of the week and a column for each broad category.

2. Just after you complete a task, write down how long it took you to finish it. If you spent an hour on Tuesday morning responding to emails, for example, record that in the Administrative Tasks column, and so on.

TABLE 1

Time-tracking tool

Week ending 4/14	Core responsibilities	Personal growth	Managing people	Crisis and fires	Free time	Administrative tasks	Total time/ day
Monday	2 hrs	1 hr	3 hrs	0 hrs	0 hrs	2 hrs	8 hrs
Tuesday	3	1	4	0	0	2	10
Wednesday	7	0	0	1	0	2	10
Thursday	0	3	3	0	0	2	8
Friday	1	2	0	1	3	2	9
Total time/ activity	13 hrs	7 hrs	10 hrs	2 hrs	3 hrs	10 hrs	45 hrs
% of time	29%	16%	22%	4%	7%	22%	100%

3. At the end of each day, take five minutes or so to tally the total amount of time that you spent on each activity. Do the same at the end of the week as well.

4. Next, calculate the percentage of your work-week that you spent on each activity.

5. Finally, visualize the results by creating a pie chart (figure 1). (You easily can do so using

FIGURE 1

Time-tracking chart

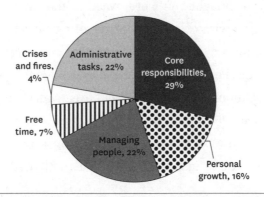

Excel's chart functions.) You'll be able to see which activities are taking up the biggest chunk of your time.

Examine your results

As you go, be on the lookout for patterns and habits: Identifying these is the point of the exercise. Most likely, your results don't align with the objectives you outlined initially. Maybe you'll realize that you're spending much more time on administrative tasks than you thought you were, wasting too much time socializing with colleagues, or devoting far less time developing a new strategy for your business unit than you'd like. Perhaps you thought you weren't spending that much time on a particular category, but you really are. Or it could be the other way around: You bemoan how much time you spend on a particular task but you've just realized that it's not that much compared with your other categories. You may find that you're spending more time than you expected on non-work-related activities.

You may also have uncovered some more nuanced patterns and habits as well. Say you tend to unwind for 30 minutes after a meeting, or you often get drawn into overly long conversations by a chatty colleague, or your productivity tends to tail off each day around 3 p.m.

Recognizing patterns large and small will inform the kinds of changes you will make in how you spend your time.

If you have the flexibility, you can use this data to make more creative and well-informed decisions about what to do with your time. Even if you have little to no control over your day-to-day schedule, it can help you structure a get-real conversation with your manager. Numbers help: If you can show her that you are spending 10 hours a week on a task that isn't a strategic priority, she may be able to help you shift your responsibilities.

Unearthing these issues means that you know where to shift your priorities and where to make improvements. Now you need a plan to help make that happen.

Develop a Plan

Develop a Plan

In the next stage—the planning stage—you'll take what you learned from time tracking and develop the plan you need to spend your time more wisely in the future.

Reclaim your time

You now have a good idea of which kinds of work are taking the most and the least of your time, and a general sense of how those realities measure up against the goals you've set. The next step is to find more time to spend on your highest-priority activity.

Say your goal is to improve your people management, but your time-tracking metrics reveal you've been spending only an hour per week on people-management-related tasks—not nearly enough. To meet your goal, you'll need to devote more time, energy, and resources to it. But how much? Three hours? Five?

Start by thinking about what tasks you'll need to perform in order to reach your goal. You will probably want to interact more often with your eight direct reports. One way to do this is to schedule weekly, half-hour check-ins with each of them, for a total of four hours. You may also want to think more seriously about planning some training for them—that will probably take another half hour per week.

Next, figure out where you'll get those extra three and a half hours. Chances are that you don't have that much free time available, so you'll have to spend less time doing other things. Identifying where to cut can be tricky—you'll want to make the *right* trade-offs.

Even though your overall objective is to spend more time on your most important activities, you may not have that many low-value tasks to jettison. Of course you can free up some time by cleaning up some of the bad habits, inefficiencies, and time sinks that you uncovered when tracking your time—such as those thirty minutes you use to unwind after meetings. But some decisions may be more difficult, requiring you to compromise, or revisit, your goals if you can't "find" enough time.

Most likely, it's going to take some work to figure out. But take your best guess. You can lock in a more realistic number when you take a closer look at the rest of your job categories, which we'll cover next.

Create a big-picture vision

The next step is to apply this process of reallocating time more broadly to your other job categories—

which will require some prioritizing of your tasks. You'll also put some interim goals in place to ensure your success. This may seem like overkill, especially if redistributing your time to your highest-priority activity was a straightforward process, but it's worth the effort because it's rare that your top priority category is the only one you need to attend to.

Here's how to do it:

- *Prioritize.* First, rank all of your time-tracked categories in order of priority (by how important they are—not the amount of time you're currently spending on them) and place them in the far left column—highest on top, lowest on bottom as shown in table 2.

- *Allocate time.* Now determine how much time you can spend on each category. You've already done this for your highest-priority category. Moving down the list, allocate time to your other categories as well. Of course, you only have so many hours in your week. If you add a

TABLE 2

Big-picture vision

Job category	Goals	% time required	Hours/ workweek	Key activities
Managing people	• Take a more active role in my team's growth and development • Develop a better relationship with my boss	25%	10	• Meet with direct reports on a weekly basis • Arrange for training for my team • Meet with boss biweekly
Personal growth	• Expand my finance knowledge	23%	9	• Take online finance class
Core responsibilities	• Reach personal and corporate goals for this fiscal year	32%	13	• Develop a more direct relationship with customers • Draft a new strategic plan for my business unit
Administrative tasks	• Be more efficient at email	13%	5	• Set aside one hour a day for less important and non-urgent emails
Crises and fires	• Learn to prioritize and delegate better	5%	2	• Develop a plan to prioritize interruptions based on importance and urgency • Delegate less important "emergencies" to others
Free time	• Take meaningful breaks throughout the day	3%	1	• Go for three walks a week
Totals:		100%	40	

few hours to one category, you'll need to take them away from another. If you're very busy, you may only be able to adjust your time allotments by a few hours or so. Even that will help.

This step may take you a few rounds to get right. As you review your list, you may realize that you'll need to devote more time to some categories than you'd anticipated. In that case, lower your time allocations in one or more other categories to make up the difference. If you're lucky, you may discover that you can devote less time to something. Then simply allocate the extra time to one of your highest-priority categories.

Note also that your highest priorities, no matter how important they are, will probably take up only a small fraction of your schedule. That's OK. The objective isn't to spend the majority of your time on these tasks; it's to find *enough* time to ensure that you reach your goals.

Finally, give yourself some breathing room as you build out your schedule; you may want

to save a few hours each week to deal with
unanticipated activities, such as lunch with
a former colleague who's in town.

- *Establish interim goals.* Once you have reallo-
cated your time, it's useful to set goals—interim
milestones—in each of your job categories.
What do you need to accomplish in a month,
quarter, or year? Make sure that these goals
match up with any that your manager has made
for you, as you did when considering your overall goals at the beginning of this process.

   Save your most ambitious goals for your
high-priority categories since you'll want to devote the bulk of your time, focus, and energy to
them. It's still useful to set goals for your other
categories as well, however. They'll keep you
focused and motivated.

- *Identify key tasks.* List the tasks that you'll
need to complete in order to achieve those goals
and place them in the next column. If you know

the specific steps that you plan on taking, you're more likely to meet your goals; having more actionable tasks will make it easier to hold yourself accountable. You either complete them or you don't: There's no fudging it.

Table 2 is an example of what a big-picture vision should look like. Your job categories, time allocations, goals, and key tasks will probably differ from the ones shown here, but if you follow the basic steps described above, you'll have no trouble mapping out a realistic and attainable plan of your own.

Do a reality check

Your goals and time allotments may seem reasonable on paper, but once you get into the flow of a workweek, you may find that they're unrealistic. Perhaps you failed to account for just how much time you spend on a particular task, or how long it takes you to transition between activities, or maybe you even forgot about a category that doesn't come up very frequently, such as a quarterly report, or annual performance evaluations. The next chapter will show you how to put your plan into action, but as you do so it will be important for you to closely track your progress—by continuing to track your time—for a week or two.

Depending on what you discover, you may need to tweak your time allotments, adjust your goals, or both. Don't worry: That's par for the course. Just start at the bottom of your list—with your low-value tasks—and see if you can scale down your goals.

You can't do everything, so don't spread yourself too thin. The purpose of time management, isn't to find ways to do more work; it's to get the *right* work done while working at a consistent and comfortable pace. The more realistic, reasonable, and attainable your plan is, the more successful you'll be at managing your time.

Execute Your Plan: Time Boxing

Execute Your Plan: Time Boxing

You've tracked your time, and you've developed a detailed plan to spend it more wisely. The next step is putting your plan into action and sticking to it. You'll do this using a tool called time boxing.

Execution is by far the hardest part of the time-management process. When you're juggling a wide range of tasks, goals, responsibilities, meetings, and deadlines, it's not easy to stick to a plan, no matter how carefully crafted it is. But if you take a more disciplined, thoughtful, and organized approach to your daily schedule, it *is* possible to stay on track.

Time-boxing basics

Time boxing is a planning tool that's a cross between a calendar and a to-do list. It involves breaking down your schedule into a number of small time periods—say, in half-hour, hour-long, or two-hour-long chunks—and then slotting tasks into each chunk. It's like scheduling meetings with yourself: Set the agenda, set the time, and show up on time prepared to work.

One of the benefits of time boxing—other than forcing you to be realistic about what work you can accomplish when, and making sure you have the time to do it—is that it helps you group similar tasks so you can take advantage of any efficiencies. Think about a trip to the grocery store. If you had a list of 25 items (meat, milk, vegetables, cereal, cheese, yogurt, rice, coffee, etc.), you wouldn't zigzag from aisle 1 to aisle 15, then aisle 2, aisle 9, aisle 5, and back to aisle 15.

You'd separate the items based on their proximity to each other, and then work sequentially from one end of the store to the other, picking up two or three items from each aisle as you go.

Typically, when it comes to tackling our to-do lists for work, we're more like that zigzagging shopper: We don't always go about things as rationally as we would if we stopped to plan. Instead we blindly attack whatever's on top of that arbitrarily constructed list without thinking about the most logical and efficient sequence. We fail to take into account the value, importance, and priority level of every task. So, like the shopper, we end up zigzagging from one activity to the next and back again. Time boxing prevents that kind of randomness and instead brings the following:

- *Accountability*. Scheduling in advance when and how long you're going to work on a task gives you the best chance of making sure you'll devote the right amount of time to your most important activities. If you commit a schedule to paper, you're more likely to follow it.

- *Efficiency.* Grouping similar tasks together will allow you to get more done in less time because you won't be shifting mental gears between tasks.

- *Time awareness.* You'll be more focused and productive when you know you're on the clock, and you'll be less likely to give away that time to a last-minute meeting or a chat with a coworker.

- *Healthy pressure.* When you know you only have a set period of time to accomplish something, you're more likely to push ahead and get it done. If you're driven by deadlines, this method gives you more of them.

- *Focus.* An hour you intend to spend on a task can quickly turn into two or three if your energy levels go down or if you're distracted. But when you set time constraints, you're more likely to keep your attention on the project at hand.

- *Effectiveness.* Do you spend too much time tweaking emails or slide decks once they're essentially complete? There's nothing wrong with trying to get something right, but sometimes good enough is good enough. Setting a time limit will help to quell the urge to spend too much time on minor, inconsequential details and force you to see the big picture instead.

You can adapt time boxing to your needs and preferences. If your job has a lot of moving parts—that is, if you need to manage a lot of competing responsibilities, deadlines, and projects—then you may find that you'll want to plan every task, activity, and project. If your schedule is relatively stable, you may choose to use it just for specific categories of work, say, to block off time for administrative tasks.

Setting up your time boxes

Here's how to create your time-boxing system. Table 3 shows an example.

1. *Review your week.* One day a week—say, Friday afternoon or Monday morning—review the week ahead. Deadlines, commitments, meetings, tasks: Take an inventory of everything that you need to accomplish.

2. *Prioritize the items on the list.* Put the deadline-sensitive tasks first, your goal-oriented tasks second, and then schedule these around your recurring tasks and obligations. This step is the most important, so give it the attention it warrants. We'll cover this in more depth in the next section.

3. *Estimate time for tasks.* Calculate how long you think each task will take you to complete.

If you're new to time boxing, it's a good idea to err on the side of caution. It's much better to overestimate than underestimate, so include some slack time in your calculations.

4. *Slot time boxes into your calendar.* Create a series of time boxes, spreading them throughout your calendar. You can enter them directly into your calendaring software (such as Outlook or Google Calendar) or first sketch them out on a piece of paper. But you'll want to end up making a note of them wherever you keep track of your appointments so you treat them with the same degree of rigor.

5. *Review your estimates.* Always keep track of the accuracy of your time estimates after the fact. Note the tasks that you finished and the ones that you didn't. This will help you make better estimates in the future.

TABLE 3

Time-boxing tool

Adapt this to any type of calendar or software program.

Schedule for Monday and Tuesday mornings

Time	Monday	Tuesday
8:00 a.m.	**Task:** Research strategic plan (SP) **Actual time spent:**	**Task:** Research SP; call Joe **Actual time spent:**
9:00 a.m.	**Task:** Monday staff meeting **Actual time spent:**	**Task:** Follow up on new leads **Actual time spent:**
10:00 a.m.	**Task:** Plan to delegate invoicing task **Actual time spent:**	**Task:** Meet with Joe about his sales figures **Task:** Review résumés for administrative assistant position **Actual time spent:**
11:00 a.m.	**Task:** Return phone calls and email messages **Actual time spent:**	**Task:** Work with Jane **Actual time spent:**

How to prioritize tasks

When setting a daily schedule, one of the most critical questions is which tasks to do first, second, third, and so on. Many of us skip thinking this through, but when we do, we often do the wrong work at the wrong time—and so we spend more time than we should on things that matter less.

Sometimes, for example, we choose one task over another because it's easier or because it gives us instant gratification, even though we have more important work to do. Or we work on all our big projects but let smaller tasks slip through the cracks. We aren't necessarily doing this deliberately; on a daily basis, we face hundreds, if not thousands, of choices, and it's difficult to keep the big picture in mind at all times.

Even if we're trying to be careful, it can be hard to decide what to tackle next. Do you work on the minor task that has a deadline today or the major project that isn't due for another few weeks? Is it so bad to seize low-hanging fruit?

Developing a system to prioritize your tasks will simplify your decision-making process and will encourage you to make better decisions on a more consistent basis.

The following two-by-two matrix—popularized by productivity expert Stephen Covey—will help you prioritize your tasks based on their importance and urgency. When examining an item on your to-do list or assessing a new task that you've just been assigned, decide if it's urgent (needs to be done soon) or not urgent, and whether it's important (will have a big impact) or unimportant, and then apply these preestablished rules.

1. *Urgent and important.* These are the crises and deadlines that you have to deal with throughout the course of the week. Say there's a problem with a product that you oversee, the website that you help maintain, or a big client that you handle. These should always be your highest priority.

2. *Not urgent but important.* This quadrant consists of tasks that have a high impact on you or your organization but aren't necessarily time

sensitive. These tasks are likely to be closely related to your long-term goals: acquisition of a new skill or working on a big project, for example. Since they're not urgent, we often fail to devote enough time to them. That's why you should make them your second priority.

3. *Urgent but less important.* These tasks need to be done quickly, but have a lower impact if they're not done at all or if they're late. When considering whether something is less important, weigh not only its potential impact on you but on your group or organization as well. These should be your third priority.

4. *Not urgent and less important.* The name says it all. These are the tasks that don't require immediate attention and aren't urgent. These should be your last priority. Some email management may fall into this category, for example.

By using these priorities to help guide your schedule, you'll be more likely to do the right work at the right time.

Time boxing is an iterative process, so it won't always be perfect. Your estimates will be off sometimes, and your schedule may change more quickly and dramatically than you'd like. But the more seriously you take the time you've set aside for your work, and the priorities you set, the more realistic your schedule will be, and the more likely it will be that you can get your most important and urgent work done.

Keep Yourself on Track

Keep Yourself on Track

Good time management is based on preparation. Once you establish goals, set priorities, and develop a plan, it will be easier to stick with it. But, as you can probably guess, even if you invest time in preparing, it won't always be easy. It doesn't matter if you're extremely organized and self-disciplined; you're going to find yourself in trouble from time to time. There will be roadblocks along the way, and you may fall back into bad habits.

Common weak spots and challenges that cause us to deviate from our well-intentioned plans include deadlines, a proclivity for procrastination, and interruptions—including email and meetings. Manage each of these well and you'll be on your way to staying on track.

Manage your deadlines

Deadlines for big projects can be daunting. This is especially true if you have a lot of other work on your plate (and who ever has just one project?). Your schedule, your colleagues, and your project may suffer if you don't manage the deadline well.

If you fail to set aside adequate time to complete a project, and the deadline is approaching at a fast clip, you'll have to drop everything else at once. The project, whether you like it or not, is now your most urgent and important task (and, suddenly, the most urgent and important tasks for others involved in the project who are depending on you). The rest of your to-do list will need to wait—no matter what important items remain on it. And if there's a last-minute change to the project, or you get a surprise assignment that's unrelated, you may be left without options other than missing your deadline.

On the other hand, the better you are at preparing for deadlines, the more reliable and effective you will be at doing your job.

Here's how to make deadlines doable.

Plan from the beginning

Does the following scenario sound familiar? When you originally got the assignment, you made a quick mental note, a guess really, about how long the project might take to complete, and then you didn't give it a second thought. But now that you've started it, the truth hits you. What you thought would take a few days to finish is going to take you a week or two, and you're going to miss your deadline.

This situation is easy to avoid with some disciplined planning. When you're first given a deadline, always take the time to estimate how long the work will really take you to complete. Think about how you will do it: Will you break it out into pieces? Are there logical stages—perhaps some that depend on others' contributions or feedback? Once you understand all the tasks involved and have estimated how long they will take, work backward from the due date and set yourself smaller deadlines along the way. Give yourself enough time to get it all done at a calm and comfortable pace.

It may sound silly to do this for small tasks, but even then it will help you be realistic about what you will need to accomplish when. So be disciplined about doing this with each assignment you get.

Sequence big to small

If you can, it's also helpful to sequence your project so that each successive subtask is shorter and easier than the last—that is, start with the most difficult and time-sensitive tasks, and end with the least.

Sequencing allows you to get the hardest and most time-consuming parts of a project out of the way first. This should keep your motivation high throughout the process—by the time you're finished with the first few tasks, the rest is easy! It will also prevent you from stalling near the finish line, since you're not leaving the toughest work for last.

Sequencing also allows you to track your progress against the deadline you're trying to meet. Say you're three weeks into a six-week assignment, and you've completed half the tasks on your list. Because you front-loaded your schedule with the most challenging and time-consuming tasks, you can be confident that you'll meet your deadline, since the second half of your list should take you less time to finish than the first.

If you find yourself behind schedule, you'll know to adjust your estimates and to allocate more time to the project going forward. As long as you catch it early on, your deadline should still be within reach.

Overcome procrastination

We all put off work—usually more so the more we dread actually doing that particular task.

That's not always a bad thing. If the work is un-important and non-urgent, it *should* be low on your list of priorities in the first place, after all. But when you have the choice to do (a) more important work, (b) less important work, or (c) nothing at all, and you consistently pick (b) or (c), procrastination can be-come a real problem.

Understanding why you're procrastinating can help you stop. Often it's because either the task is something that you don't want to do, that you're not good at doing, or that you find too daunting. When-ever you feel the urge to procrastinate, ask yourself if one of those reasons is the culprit.

Once you pinpoint the cause, use one of these remedies.

- *Set deadlines.* Deadlines hold you accountable, so they're particularly helpful if you just don't want to do something. Deadlines work for larger projects that are too daunting as well: Just break the project down into smaller tasks, and set a deadline for each. Each chunk will be easier to approach, and you know when you need to complete it, so you'll be less likely to put it off. (See more on starting small below.)

- *Start small.* When we don't want to do something, especially a big and difficult task, dread can sink in, and procrastination rears its ugly head. More often than not, however, the dread dissipates when we actually get down to work. The key is to start small. If you're dreading giving a presentation, for example—all that preparation, not to mention the public speaking—don't imagine that you have to tackle the prep work all at once. Do some research, take notes, or brainstorm. Consider it a warm-up of sorts. Once you're comfortable, you'll be more apt to jump into the rest of the project without trepidation.

- *Ask for help.* If you're having trouble with something, ask a colleague for assistance rather than postponing your work on it. It sounds like common sense, but our coworkers are a resource that many of us don't utilize enough; instead we struggle, get stuck, and then put the work aside (because somehow later it will be easier?). But if a colleague can provide you with a quick answer or point you in the right direction, or even listen to you talk through your thinking on something, you'll get the task done, you'll learn something, and you'll help build a relationship with this individual.

- *Make it a game.* We also procrastinate if a task provides us with little to no satisfaction, such as filing or filling out expense reports. We dislike doing these tasks, and once we finish them, we don't experience a buzz of accomplishment. So make a game out of it: Group a bunch of your menial tasks together, set a timer for 15 or 20 minutes, and get to work. If the tasks require more thought and attention, and your time limit isn't wise, you can always challenge yourself to improve.

Avoid interruptions

Not all interruptions—from non-urgent emails to crises—are created equal, but sometimes we treat them as if they were. We get caught up in the rush, and respond to everything right away regardless of its importance and urgency.

Give yourself some ground rules to ensure that if your attention is being diverted, you are making the right choice about what to focus on at that time. Here are some rules of thumb:

- If the problem is urgent and important, take care of it as soon as possible. Yes, it will steal your focus from the task at hand, but as discussed in the previous chapter, this category of concerns should be your highest priority.

- If the problem doesn't need immediate attention and it's going to take up more than a few minutes of your time, then move it to a time box that you've dedicated for less urgent work.

- If none of the options above are viable, refer the interrupting person to a colleague who could also handle his or her problem as well as— maybe even better—than you could.

Email

We all have a love/hate relationship with email. It's an efficient way to communicate, but it can also eat up a lot of time, especially if you open and respond to each and every message right away.

Some of the push and pull of email is unavoidable. If you work in a client-based or customer-centric business, for example, you may need to keep a close eye on your inbox all day long. But think hard about whether the nature of your work really requires you to be "on" all the time. If not, there's no reason to drop what you're doing every time you receive an email—especially if you're focused on another task. Sure, you want to be responsive and alert, but you also don't want to be in reaction mode all day. It will kill your focus.

Email can provide a refuge from more difficult tasks, so it is easy for it to turn into a time-wasting trap: First you answer one non-urgent email, then another, then another, then another. If this occurs multiple times an hour—which is very common—you'll end up taking valuable time away from more important work.

If you find yourself accidentally surrendering more time to new message notifications than you'd like, try dedicating small blocks of time each day to email.

First thing in the morning, every hour, before or after lunch, or right before you call it a night—these are all great times to respond to non-urgent messages.

Remember: Your objective is to devote as much focus, energy, and time as possible to the things that are most important to you. By restricting the times during which you can be distracted by email, you'll allow yourself more time for uninterrupted work.

Meetings

Meetings, especially if you're a manager, can take up a large amount of your day. But when you're shuttling from conference room to conference room for hours at a time, it's hard to get important work done.

Meetings do serve important purposes: They keep everyone informed, solicit critical points of view, and even encourage social interaction. But some meetings fail to meet those goals; they're superfluous and inefficient. Those are the meetings to watch out for.

Whether you "own" meetings or whether you're just an attendee, consider whether the time you're spending in conference rooms is valuable—more so than the other work you could be doing in that time. If you run meetings:

- Don't always default to an hour-long meeting time. Sometimes the agenda only warrants a half hour or less. Consider scheduling a 20-minute or a 50-minute meeting so you and your attendees can complete follow-up tasks within the remaining 10 minutes.

- Cancel an instance of a recurring meeting—say, a weekly staff meeting—if you don't have an agenda.

- If you're scheduling a meeting to share information, consider whether a simple email would be an adequate option. Reserve meetings for items that require a direct response from team members, or if the matter is sensitive enough that attendees will want to hear from you in person (but not so sensitive that it should be handled one-on-one).

If you are a meeting invitee:

- Be more selective when accepting meeting invitations. Ask yourself this question: If you were to call in sick the day of the meeting, would it need to be rescheduled? If the answer is no, then you may be able to decline it. This can be risky, however. The other participants may make important decisions without you, or a higher-up may notice your absence. You can mitigate some of these risks by getting approval from your boss or the meeting leader beforehand and following up with the important parties after the meeting to see if they need your input on any of the discussion points.

- If you're swamped with work and need some
  breathing room, evaluate the meetings already
  on your calendar. Do you have an instance of a
  recurring meeting that doesn't have an agenda
  posted? Are there any meetings you could skip
  or move? Don't assume that just because a
  meeting is on your calendar that that time is in-
  violable. However, if you're declining a meeting
  after accepting it, verify with the organizer that
  your role in the meeting is not critical—and as
  a common courtesy to let him or her know you
  won't be there—and follow up with colleagues
  later that day, or ask to see the meeting notes if
  you need to catch up.

Meetings can be difficult to manage because they're
often beyond your control. Unless you own the meeting, you don't decide its time or length or what's cov-
ered. But know that you can make more constructive
choices. You're valuable to your organization because

of the quality of your work, not the number of meeting invitations that you accept. Being more selective about which meetings you attend reflects your ability to prioritize and manage your time well.

Think on your feet

These traps and roadblocks are ever-present in our work lives; you won't be able to completely avoid them. But if you're always on the lookout for them, and have a solid plan in place for dealing with them, you'll do a better job making good time-management decisions as these challenges come up, and get back on track as quickly as possible.

Reassess Yourself

Reassess Yourself

Time management isn't a once-and-done process. Even if you track your time, follow a detailed and smart plan, time box your tasks, and avoid common pitfalls, continue to assess and reassess your progress.

As your priorities shift and your schedule evolves, you'll need to be both persistent and responsive in order to stay on track. These two characteristics are what separate great time managers from good ones. Great time managers don't just prepare and then stick to their plans; they are also able to improvise. They learn from their mistakes, and make adjustments.

Are you still on track?

It's easy to get caught up in the day-to-day hustle of our work lives. We can lose track of our big-picture goals. So it's important to slow down to make sure our priorities still line up with those objectives.

The best way to do this is to schedule self-check-ups. Think of these as you would a trip to the doctor. Is everything working well? Are there warning signs that you should be worried about? Are there things you need to improve?

The frequency of your check-ups will depend on your situation. If you're juggling multiple projects and deadlines, you may want to assess yourself each week, every few days, or even at the end of each day. If you're checking off every item on your to-do lists, meeting deadlines, hitting milestones, and finding ample time to work on the projects, tasks, and skills that mean the most to you, then a once-a-month check-in will probably suit you fine.

A check-up gives you a chance to identify warning signs and areas that need improvement before it's too late, so that you can change your plan or shift your priorities. Even if you're in good shape, a frequent check-up will, at the very least, give you the peace of mind that your plan is working well.

When checking up, ask yourself these questions:

- Do I feel prepared and focused each day?

- Do I feel like I have enough time to get everything done?

- Am I completing my scheduled tasks?

- Am I making reasonable progress each week?

- Do I frequently work at a comfortable, non-frenzied pace?

- Are my time estimates more accurate than before?

- Am I meeting deadlines?

- Am I achieving my goals?

These questions should get you started. But feel free to add your own to the list. If you have a particular weakness—say, procrastination—it's a good idea to assess how well you're improving in that area as well.

Getting back on track

Your answers to the check-up questions will determine your course of action.

- *On track.* If you answered "yes" to most of the questions, that means you're on the right track. That's great! Keep up with what you're doing, and make adjustments as you see fit.

   Even though everything is going well, take the time to write down anything that you learned since your last check-up. If you miscalculated how long a project would take to complete, for example, make a note of it so you don't make the same mistake twice. Time management is a continual learning process. You may fail sometimes, but as long as you learn something in the process, you'll make better decisions in the future. This is the time to capture that learning so you can put it into action when the next opportunity arises.

- *Off track.* If you answered "no" to several of these questions, then you may need to make a few modifications. Some of the changes may be obvious. If you're not meeting deadlines, you may be able to fix the problem by adding more time to your estimates in the future. But some may take more work to figure out. If you're not on track to meet your overarching goals, for example, you may have to do some soul searching.

  A good place to start is the big-picture vision you created—your priorities, goals, and time allocations. Did you set your goals too high?

Are your time allocations off? Did you set your priorities correctly?

If you miscalculated or overlooked something, don't worry: These things are hard to gauge and will often take some adjusting. When this happens, realistically lower your goals, tweak your time allotments, or rerank your priorities.

If you're still at a loss, try tracking your time again. You may have missed something the first time, your workload may have increased, or you may have picked up some new bad habits.

Whether you're on track or off track, the important thing is to keep learning. So make some changes. Strive to get better. Assess and reassess. As long as you prepare, plan, prioritize, and pivot when needed, you will grow into an effective time manager.

Sources

Birkinshaw, Julian, and Jordan Cohen. "Make Time for the Work That Matters." *Harvard Business Review*, September 2013. (product #R1309K).

Bregman, Peter. "A Better Way to Manage Your To-Do List." HBR Blog Network, February 24, 2011. http://blogs.hbr.org/2011/02/a-better-way-to-manage-your-to/.

Cardwell, Lynda. "Making the Most of 'Slow Time.'" *Harvard Management Update*, September 2003. http://blogs.hbr.org/2008/02/making-the-most-of-slow-time-1/.

Find Your Focus: Get Things Done the Smart Way. HBR OnPoint Magazine, November 2013.

Harvard Business School Publishing. Harvard Manage-Mentor. Boston: Harvard Business School Publishing, 2002.

Harvard Business School Publishing. *HBR Guide to Getting the Right Work Done*. Boston: Harvard Business Review Press, 2012.

Sources

Harvard Business School Publishing. *Pocket Mentor: Managing Time.* Boston: Harvard Business School Press, 2006.

Saunders, Elizabeth Greene. "Break Your Addiction to Meetings." HBR Blog Network, February 2013. http://blogs.hbr.org/2013/02/break-your-addiction-to-meetin/.

Learn More

Recent research

Birkinshaw, Julian, and Jordan Cohan. "Make Time for the Work That Matters." *Harvard Business Review*, September 2013 (product #R1309K).

Birkinshaw and Cohan's article reveals just how much time knowledge workers can save by eliminating and delegating unimportant tasks so that they can replace them with value-added ones. The authors outline a process that professionals can follow to identify those unnecessary tasks; drop, delegate, or redesign them; and then allocate freed-up time for more valuable work. The article includes an interactive self-assessment.

Mogilner, Cassie. "You'll Feel Less Rushed If You Give Time Away." *Harvard Business Review*, September 2012 (product #F1209D).

In this Q&A article Mogilner shares her research, which reveals that offering your time to others could make you actually feel less rushed and that you have more time on your hands.

Classics

Billington, Jim. "Fairly Timeless Insights on How to Manage Your Time." *Harvard Management Update*, February 1997 (product #U97020).

Too much literature on time management stresses how to do more faster—essentially how to manage a to-do list. Instead, as Billington argues in this newsletter article, managers should visualize the end result by "getting on the balcony—seeing the whole field of play and where their undertaking should fit in." People should spend most of their time on work that is truly important, and avoid the addiction to urgency—fighting fires, fielding calls, firing off memos, and attending irrelevant meetings that can consume a manager's day but add little lasting value. A short checklist of practical tips to increase efficiency is included.

Blanchard, Kenneth, William Oncken Jr., and Hal Burrows. *The One Minute Manager Meets the Monkey*. New York: Quill, 1989.

The message in this book is to let your direct reports take on the tasks they can and should do. Trust them and train them, but don't do it yourself!

Mackenzie, Alec, and Pat Nickerson. *The Time Trap: The Classic Book on Time Management*. 4th ed. New York: American Management Association, 2009.

Nickerson updates Mackenzie's classic book of "time traps" that keep us from being as productive as we'd like. The authors diagnose each trap—such as "the inability to say no" and "poor delegation and training"—and then give advice for how to avoid it.

Morgenstern, Julie. *Time Management from the Inside Out: The Foolproof System for Taking Control of Your Schedule and Your Life.* 2nd ed. New York: Henry Holt, 2004.

Those who fear "time management" because they worry about living uncreative or overly scheduled lives will find themselves reassured by Morgenstern's ability to customize her system. The most important thing readers must do, she emphasizes in this book, is to create a time-management system that fits their personal style—whether it be spontaneous and easily distracted or highly regimented and efficient.

Oncken, William Jr., and Donald L. Wass. "Management Time: Who's Got the Monkey?" *Harvard Business Review* OnPoint Enhanced Edition. Boston: Harvard Business School Publishing, 2000.

Many managers feel overwhelmed. They have too many problems—too many monkeys—on their backs. All too often, they find themselves running out of time while their subordinates are running out of work. Such is the common phenomenon described by the late William Oncken Jr. and Donald L. Wass in this 1974 HBR classic. This article describes how the manager can reverse this phenomenon and delegate effectively. In his accompanying commentary, Stephen R. Covey discusses both the enduring power of this message and how theories of time management have progressed beyond these ideas.

Peters, Thomas J. "Leadership: Sad Facts and Silver Linings." *Harvard Business Review* OnPoint Enhanced Edition. Boston: Harvard Business School Publishing, 2001 (product #8326).

In this article Peters suggests that the "sad facts" of managerial life can be turned into opportunities to communicate values and to persuade. The fragmented nature of the executive's workday can also create a succession of opportunities to tackle bits of the issue stream. The fragmentation is precisely what permits a manager to fine-tune, test, and retest the strategic signals being sent to the company.

Index

Index

Notes

Notes

Notes

Notes

Notes

Notes

Notes

Notes

Notes

Notes

Notes

Notes

Notes

Notes

Notes

Notes